WITCH TRIALS

Gareth Stevens
Publishing

Alix Wood

Please visit our website, **www.garethstevens.com**. For a free color catalog of all our high-quality books, call toll free 1-800-542-2595 or fax 1-877-542-2596

Library of Congress Cataloging-in-Publication Data

Wood, Alix.
Witch trials / by Alix Wood.
  p. cm. — (Why'd they do that? strange customs of the past)
Includes index.
ISBN 978-1-4339-9593-4 (pbk.)
ISBN 978-1-4339-9594-1 (6-pack)
ISBN 978-1-4339-9592-7 (library binding)
1. Witchcraft—Juvenile literature. 2. Trials (Witchcraft)—Juvenile literature. I. Wood, Alix. II. Title.
GR530.W66 2014
398.352—dc23

First Edition

Published in 2014 by
Gareth Stevens Publishing
111 East 14th Street, Suite 349
New York, NY 10003

© Alix Wood Books

Produced for Gareth Stevens by Alix Wood Books
Designed and illustrated by Alix Wood
Picture and content research: Kevin Wood
Editor: Eloise Macgregor
Consultant: Rupert Matthews, the History Man

Photo credits: Cover, © Fotolia; 4 © William A. Crafts; 10, 12, 13 inset © Public Domain; 15 inset © Dominique Jacquin; 17 inset © Public Domain; 18 © Henrietta D. Kimball; 20 © Paul van Somer/The Royal Collection; 21 top © Alix Wood; 21 bottom © Public Domain; 22 © Rosenwald Collection/nga; 24 top © Tom Oates; 24 bottom © Dr Greg; 26 © Public Domain; 29 © Veton PICQ; 1, 3, 5, 7, 8, 9, 13 main, 15 bottom, 16, 19, 23, 28 © Shutterstock

Printed in the United States of America

CPSIA compliance information: Batch #CS13GS: For further information contact Gareth Stevens, New York, New York at 1-800-542-2595.-

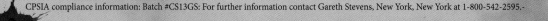

Contents

What's a Witch Trial?

In medieval Europe and in the colonial period in North America, many people believed in witches and witchcraft. People thought to be witches were tried by the courts and could be sentenced to death. As there is no such thing as a witch, it is interesting that so many people were found guilty!

Witches were believed to worship the devil. People believed witches could be the cause of any bad luck that affected the community. They could be blamed for crop failure, death, illness, or any other misfortune. Both men and women were accused of witchcraft. People accused of witchcraft were usually put on trial to judge if they were guilty. Sometimes the witches had to undergo tests to prove their guilt or innocence.

An engraving of a Salem witch trial

Most witch hunts in Europe took place between about 1580 and 1630. The Salem witch hunts in North America were between 1692 and 1693. Across the world, 12,545 executions as a result of witch trials were recorded, but it is believed the total was much higher, with most experts thinking that closer to 40,000 people were executed.

REALLY?

During the medieval period, there was widespread belief in magic across Europe. Those accused of being witches were often people who performed folk magic, a popular practice amongst ordinary people. They would perform simple charms and spells.

LOST IN TRANSLATION?

The witch trials used a passage from the book of Exodus in the Bible to back up their executions. It states: "Thou shalt not suffer a witch to live." There is some argument over whether the word "witch" was mistranslated over the years. The Bible was originally written in Hebrew, and then translated into Greek or Latin. It was later translated into German by Martin Luther, and English translations followed. Words and concepts do not always translate well from one language to another. The word we now know as "witch" was *chasapah* in Hebrew which means "poisoner." The translation to Latin was *veneficium* which can mean "poisoning." In Latin the term *maleficos* means "witch." When it was then translated to German, the word became *Zauberinnen* which means "witch." Perhaps the English should say "poisoner," not "witch"?

A Latin translation of the Bible

How to Spot a Witch

People believed that you could tell if someone was a witch by physical signs on their bodies. There were also some tests that could be done to decide if someone was a witch. The tests don't appear to have been very fair, and a person might be found guilty even if they passed the test!

Witch-hunting was a serious business. These are some of the things people looked for when trying to spot a witch:

They are ugly old women, often with a big nose
They have pets that follow them. They talk to their pets
They make models
They hold unusual ceremonies
They are deformed in some way
They live alone and they smell
They have no shadow
They talk to themselves
They can't say certain prayers without a mistake
Their hair cannot be cut
They have red hair and green eyes
They have warts or extra fingers

6

How to Test a Witch

Weigh the witch against a stack of Bibles. If the suspected witch is heavier or lighter than the stack of Bibles, then she's guilty. If the scales balance, she's innocent!

Check for moles, birthmarks, or scars. They're marks of the devil. Try pricking one with a blade, and if it doesn't bleed or hurt, they are a witch. Some witch-hunters cheated by using knives with **retractable** blades, which obviously wouldn't draw blood.

Power over animals. If a fly or a rat entered a witch's cell while they were awaiting trial, it was believed that the witch had used her powers to make the animal do her bidding.

The swimming test. A suspected witch's right thumb was tied to the left big toe, and the left thumb to the right big toe. They were thrown in the water. If they floated, they were a witch as the devil must have helped them. If they sank, they were innocent, but had to be rescued quickly or they drowned.

REALLY?

In 1981 in Italy, a religious painting fell off the wall when Scottish nanny Carole Compton walked past. Several unexplained fires also happened in the house, so Italian police put her in prison for being a witch.

Witches' Accessories

Witches were thought to keep animals called **familiars** that help them practice their magic. Familiars were usually small animals like cats or toads. Every witch was believed to have a familiar. Pets could be considered proof that a person was a witch. Witches were also believed to ride around at night on broomsticks.

Black cats are often associated with witchcraft. A familiar could be nearly any animal, however. Other common forms are dogs, owls, and toads. Occasionally familiars could be in the shape of a human. Familiars were said to suckle blood, so witch-hunters would look for odd moles and warts to prove that a familiar had suckled from a suspected witch.

There are many superstitions involving black cats. A black cat crossing a person's path is said to be very unlucky.

Familiars were considered as dangerous as witches. They were thought to be **supernatural** beings that looked like normal animals and could spy or wreak havoc for their witch without being easily detected.

REALLY?

Women going to witches' meetings were supposed to take a broom with them. They rode the broom like a hobby horse, pretending to be knights on horseback. The brush end was the mane of the horse with the stick end trailing on the ground. People often draw it the wrong way around.

Broomstick the wrong way around

Broomstick the right way around

ANIMAL WITCH TRIALS

It was a popularly held belief during these times that the devil existed and that anyone could meet him in a forest or on a country road. Chance meetings with strangers or animals would often be explained in such a way, and unlucky events after such a meeting would be blamed on the animal. During the Salem witch trials, one man was charged with encouraging a dog to attack using magical means. The dog was tried, convicted, and hanged. Two more dogs were hung because a girl said they had given her the evil eye. A cat massacre happened in medieval Europe when all cats were thought to be a witch's familiar, so Pope Innocent VIII made a law that condemned all cats belonging to witches to death.

European Witch Trials

Witch hunts began in Europe in the early 1400s in southeastern France and western Switzerland. Soon, the idea of identifying and putting witches on trial spread to neighboring areas. The height of the European trials were between 1560 and 1630, with the large hunts first beginning in 1609.

A book called *Malleus Maleficarum* (Hammer of the Witches) was written in 1486 by a German Catholic clergyman. The book was a witch-hunt manual which helped people to identify, try, and execute witches. The book remained in use for three hundred years and had tremendous influence in the witch trials in Europe. There were several chapters that dealt specifically with **midwives**. Midwives helped women in childbirth, and they were regularly accused of witchcraft. Many people blamed any death or deformity occurring during childbirth as proof that the midwife was a witch.

Entjen Gillis was a midwife accused of killing unborn and newborn babies during the Roermond witch trials of 1613. Her arrest followed the sudden deaths of hundreds of newborns, old people, and animals. Magistrates rounded up 63 suspected witches and sentenced them all to death. Gillis was burned alive.

In some European countries, victims to be burned alive were tied to a vertical ladder and then swung down onto the fire.

THE TORSÅKER WITCH TRIALS

In 1675 in Sweden, 71 people were executed for witchcraft in a single day. About 65 of those were women, roughly one fifth of all the women in the region. The local priest, Hornaeus, made two boys stand at the door of the church to identify the witches as they came in. One boy pointed at the priest's wife, Britta Rufina, but he quickly apologized and said he had been blinded by the sun. The witches were tried and then herded up a mountain called "The Mountain of the Stake." They were beheaded away from the stakes, so they didn't drown the wood in blood and make it hard to light. Their bodies were then tied to the stakes and burned.

The Mountain of the Stake memorial stone

REALLY?

The Torsåker witnesses were mostly children because the witches were accused of abducting children on the witches' sabbath. Hornaeus had several methods to get the children to give the evidence he wanted. He whipped them, he dunked them in a frozen lake, and he put them in an oven and pretended that he would light the fire and boil them!

In Salzburg in Austria, 139 people were executed in a most unusual witch trial. Most of the victims were male beggar-children and teenagers. They were accused of black magic and supposedly led by a child called Jackl; 39 of the victims were between 10 and 14 years old.

Witch-Finder General

In England in 1644, in a village called Manningtree, the wife of a tailor named John Rivet suffered from an illness. Elizabeth Clarke, a one-legged widow, was accused of causing her illness using witchcraft. A young man called Matthew Hopkins and his colleague John Stearne investigated the accusation. This was the start of Hopkins' career as a witch-finder.

Matthew Hopkins, Witch-Finder General

Matthew Hopkins called himself "The Witch-Finder General." He was the son of a local **Puritan** minister. His beliefs made him want to rid the world of witches, but he also made a lot of money. It is believed that Hopkins was paid about £1,000 ($1,600) for his duties, which was a huge sum in those days. In Ipswich a special local tax had to be **levied** in 1645 to help pay for his services!

He kept the accused witch Elizabeth Clarke awake for three days and nights until she confessed to witchcraft. The old woman gave the names of other witches in Manningtree and the witch-hunt gathered momentum. Elizabeth was hanged. During Hopkins' witch-finding career between 1644 and 1646, he is believed to have been responsible for the deaths of 300 women.

THE WITCH HUNTER'S HANDBOOK

Matthew Hopkins published a pamphlet called *The Discovery of Witches* in 1647 where he defined witchcraft and outlined his witch-hunting methods. These methods were used later in colonial America during the Salem witch trials.

A page from The Discovery of Witches, *by Matthew Hopkins*

Matthew Hopkins turned his attention to the quiet English village of Brandeston, and its vicar of more than forty years, John Lowes. Hopkins accused Lowes of bewitching ships, which then sank. The 80-year-old denied the accusation. After four days and nights of no sleep, Lowes was finally bullied into signing a **confession**. The vicar was taken to a pond, bound hand and foot, and "swam." He survived, proving his guilt. John Lowes read out his own burial service and sermon so he could be given a Christian burial. He was then hanged. A bag of coins was given to Matthew Hopkins in payment.

Matthew Hopkins died at his home of tuberculosis on August 12, 1647, and was buried in the churchyard at Mistley Heath. One legend says Hopkins was accused of being a witch himself and was tried and drowned in the pond in the village of Mistley.

According to local legend, Hopkins' ghost is said to haunt Mistley pond.

Confessions

It is interesting that many of the accused witches in these trials confessed to their involvement. In some cases, the witches had been **tortured** or deprived of sleep to get confessions, but apparently this wasn't always the case. Sometimes the accused people would voluntarily confess. Why was this?

The strong belief that witches existed may have meant that some women wondered if they could be one. Some may have believed they were, simply because they did not behave as people around them thought they should. The witch was the opposite of a good woman, so if they were a bad woman, perhaps they were a witch.

There were many women and men who claimed to be able to do magic. They produced charms and potions to help people recover from illnesses, to cure sick animals, or to ward off bad luck. They might also threaten to hurt people using curses and black magic. Officials from the Christian churches thought that all magic used powers that came from the devil.

POSSESSED, OR ILL?

A fungus responsible for infecting rye and other cereals produces symptoms that are similar to the fits suffered by some accused witches. This disease, called ergotism, contorts a victim's body in pain, with trembling and shaking, and a twisted neck. In some cases, this is accompanied by confusion, **delusions,** and **hallucinations**. The witches were believed to be possessed by demons, but they may just have been ill.

Barley infected with the fungus that causes ergotism

REALLY?

A confession could save you. During the witch trials in Salem, if you admitted being a witch and repented, you had a very good chance of living. If you denied being a witch and insisted that you had rights which must be acknowledged, you were on a quick path to execution.

It is human nature to need explanations. Just as misfortune in a community could be blamed on witches, suspected witches could also blame their bad thoughts or bad events in their lives on demons. There are many references to infant deaths, suicides, and possible abuse in confessions of witches. It could be that people trying to make sense of bad experiences in their lives used the idea of the devil causing them as a way of explaining them to themselves.

Punishments

When someone was found guilty of witchcraft, there were a variety of punishments they could be subjected to. The punishment could depend on what country the trial took place in, or what they had used their witchcraft to do. In England, witches were usually hanged and then burned. In France, they were nearly always burned alive. Witches who refused to confess could be pressed to death by placing heavy weights on them.

This strange monument in Scotland is to Maggie Wall. No records exist of her trial or punishment, but that is not unusual. Records show that six alleged witches were executed nearby in 1663. The memorial is unusual as most victims were never given proper burials or memorials. Once convicted of witchcraft, they were no longer considered people and were laid in unmarked graves. The presence of the cross is very unusual, too, for someone said to do the devil's work!

The monument in Dunning, Scotland, says: "Maggie Wall burnt here 1657 as a witch."

REALLY?

Ordinary people accused of a crime were hanged. The upper classes were beheaded. In England in 1540, Lord Hungerford tried to use witchcraft to find out how long the king would live. He was caught and beheaded for treason.

WISER TIMES

In the 900s, before the time of witch trials, a passage in a Christian law book called *Canon Episcopi* said that it was bad to *believe* in witchcraft, not to practice it. A set of church laws from the 700s also demanded the death penalty not for the witch, but for any person who murdered an alleged witch, because believing in witches was a **pagan** superstition.

Some Gentle Witchcraft Punishments

The Pillory 	A minor first offense might mean a spell in the pillory, a wooden structure that holds the arms and head. The witch would spend six hours in her hometown pillory. The townsfolk may throw rotten vegetables at her. After a spell in jail, she may be pilloried again in different local towns until eventually released.
Head Scroll	In 1467 in England, William Byg was arrested for looking into a crystal ball. His punishment was to appear in public with a scroll on his head, a little like a dunce cap. The scroll was a symbol of a fortune teller.
Ducking 	The ducking stool was a chair attached to a wooden arm which could be swung over a river. The witch was strapped into the chair and then ducked into the river. The length of time in the water and the frequency depended on the crime of which the witch was accused.

Salem Witch Trials

In the winter of 1692, there was an outbreak of witch hysteria in the village of Salem, in colonial Massachusetts. A group of young girls began to display bizarre behavior. They suffered seizures, **blasphemous** screaming, and trance-like states when they met in the evenings in the home of Reverend Parris to listen to stories told by one of his slaves, Tituba. Doctors could find no natural cause for the disturbing behavior.

The tight-knit Puritan community decided it was the work of the devil. The village began praying and fasting in order to rid itself of the witches. The girls were pressured to reveal who controlled their behavior. Tituba confessed to seeing the devil and said that witches were everywhere in Salem. Accusations began to fly and many were charged, examined, tried, and condemned to death, including upstanding members of the congregation and a deputy constable. Even a four-year-old, Dorcas Good, was put in jail!

The parsonage in Salem Village. This photograph was taken in the late 1800s.

18

THE TRIAL OF MARTHA COREY

At Martha Corey's trial, her accusers copied the witch's every movement. If Martha shifted her feet, the girls did also. If Martha pinched her fingers, the children showed marks where they had been pinched to the magistrates and spectators. The girls told the court Martha caused them to have fits and that she kept a yellow bird that used to suck between her fingers. Martha denied everything. Martha Corey was found guilty and hanged. Her 80-year-old husband, Giles, was also accused of witchcraft. He refused to enter a plea of guilty or not guilty, in protest against the methods of the court. He was tortured by having heavy rocks placed on him until he relented. Giles died after two days of torture, three days before his wife's execution.

The hangings started in June and continued through September. Criticism of the trials grew. The convictions eventually stopped, but by then 19 victims had been hanged, one crushed to death, and five had died in prison awaiting trial. Both Tituba and another girl accuser later admitted they had been lying. Were the girls just a bit bored and making up stories, or were they really ill and thought witchcraft was to blame?

SALEM EXECUTIONS

Bridget Bishop, Rebecca Nurse, Sarah Good, Elizabeth Howe, Sarah Wildes, Susannah Martin, George Burroughs, Martha Carrier, George Jacobs, John Proctor, John Willard, Giles Corey, Martha Corey, Mary Eastey, Alice Parker, Mary Parker, Ann Pudeator, Margaret Scott, Wilmot Redd, Samuel Wardwell Sr.

Famous Witch Trials

Saints, kings, and queens have been involved in witch trials over the years. Accusing people of witchraft is often a convenient way to take away a person's power by discrediting them.

A portrait of James VI

In 1590, the witch trials in North Berwick, Scotland, involved the king. King James VI had developed a fear that witches planned to kill him after he suffered storms traveling to Denmark to claim his bride, Anne. When he returned to Scotland, the king heard of witches being tried in North Berwick and ordered the suspects to be brought to him. Several people, most notably Agnes Sampson, were convicted of using witchcraft to send storms against James's ship. James also believed the 5th Earl of Bothwell was a witch and outlawed him as a traitor. The king set up royal commissions to hunt down witches in his kingdom, recommending torture in dealing with suspects. In 1597 he wrote a book called *Daemonologie* about the evil that witches posed to society.

Anne Boleyn was Queen of England from 1533 to 1536 as the second wife of Henry VIII. Henry had Anne investigated for high treason in April 1536. She was arrested and sent to the Tower of London, where she was tried before a jury. The charges against her included witchcraft. She was beheaded four days later.

Anne Boleyn. This painting uses an original painted around 1534 as its reference. Count the fingers!

REALLY?

After Anne Boleyn's death, Nicholas Sander wanted to remove Anne's daughter Elizabeth I from the throne. In a book published in 1585, he wrote that Anne had given birth to a deformed baby, had six fingers on her right hand, a cyst under her chin and a protruding tooth—all things associated with witchcraft. It is unlikely Henry would have married her had this been true.

Her body was dug up in 1876, and no abnormalities were discovered.

JOAN OF ARC

Accusations of witchcraft were commonly made against women who lived on the margins of society. Women who were too powerful became targets as well. Joan of Arc, now the patron saint of France, was a peasant girl who experienced visions which convinced her that she was destined by God to lead the French to victory over the English. She led French forces to free the city of Orleans but was eventually taken prisoner and turned over to the English who burned her at the stake as a witch. They argued that her claims of communication with God were **heretical** and an act of disobedience to the Church.

Curses and Cures

There were few doctors in the Middle Ages, and ordinary people would seek medical help from healers who practiced herbal remedies or magic. These were often the same people that would get accused of witchcraft. Doctors that healed the sick under the guidance of the Church were acceptable, but ordinary women healing people was seen as magic, not medicine, and must be the work of the devil.

The wise woman, or witch, used herbal remedies which had been tested over years of use and claimed to use magic to give them added power. Many of the herbal remedies are still used in modern medicine today. Some of their medicines and methods were more unorthodox, but that was true of the doctors of the period too!

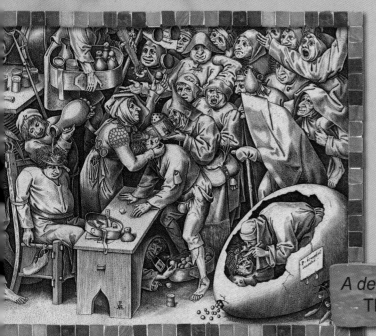

The picture on the left created in the 1500s shows a witch (in the egg shape) cutting the stones out of the head of a patient to cure madness. The assistants at the table are preparing two more patients. You can see the removed stones rolling out of the front of the egg!

A detail from an etching called
The Witch of Malleghem

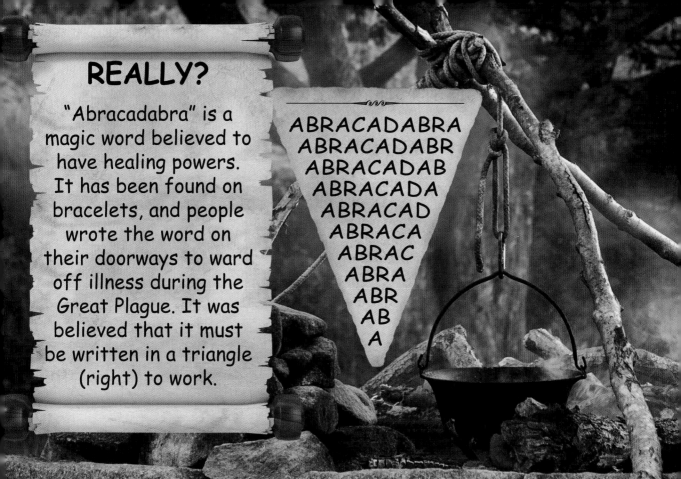

REALLY?

"Abracadabra" is a magic word believed to have healing powers. It has been found on bracelets, and people wrote the word on their doorways to ward off illness during the Great Plague. It was believed that it must be written in a triangle (right) to work.

ABRACADABRA
ABRACADABR
ABRACADAB
ABRACADA
ABRACAD
ABRACA
ABRAC
ABRA
ABR
AB
A

WITCHES' CURSES

A curse was a spell intended to cause harm. The most common way witches were thought to curse people was using an **effigy** or "poppet." A poppet was a doll made to look like the person to be harmed. It was thought that the closer the effigy resembled the victim, the more the victim would suffer when the effigy was harmed or destroyed. The burning of wax and clay figures was popularly used in curses during the Middle Ages in Europe. Sometimes they were stuck with pins, thorns, or knives. Poppets were a key piece of evidence against Bridget Bishop in the Salem witch trials. A man said he had found several poppets in the wall of the cellar in Bishop's house. Headless pins had been pushed into the poppets. Bishop was found guilty and hanged.

The Pendle Witches

The trials of the Pendle witches in 1612 are among the most famous witch trials in English history. The twelve accused lived in the area around Pendle Hill in Lancashire, and were charged with the murders of ten people by the use of witchcraft. One died in prison. And of the eleven who went to trial, ten were found guilty and executed by hanging, and one was found not guilty.

Six of the Pendle witches came from two families, the Chattoxes and the Demdikes, each headed by a woman in her eighties. Many of the allegations were made by the Demdike and Chattox families against each other. Perhaps this was because the families were rivals, both trying to make a living from healing and begging. Ann Whittle, the elderly head of the Chattox family, was executed along with her daughter Anne Redferne.

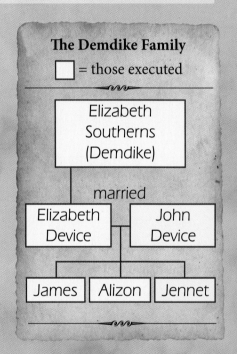

The Demdike Family

☐ = those executed

Elizabeth Southerns (Demdike)

married

Elizabeth Device — John Device

James | Alizon | Jennet

JENNET DEVICE, WITNESS AGED 9

Jennet lived with her mother, grandmother, older sister, and brother in the shadow of the Pendle Hill. Jennet's evidence in the witch trial led to the execution of 10 people, including many of her own family. She may have really thought her family was bewitched, or perhaps she had some grudge against them. At 9 years old, she probably didn't realize how serious the trial was and that her family would be killed.

Lancaster Castle, where the trials took place. The castle is still used as a court and prison today.

REALLY?

Twenty years after the Pendle trials, Jennet was accused of witchcraft, herself by 10-year-old Edmund Robinson. Edmund eventually admitted he was lying because of the stories he had heard about the Pendle witch trial. Jennet was not allowed to leave Lancaster Castle until she had paid for her board for the time she had spent there on trial!

The clerk of the court, Thomas Potts, wrote a book of all the notes he made of the trial, called *The Wonderful Discoverie of Witches in the Countie of Lancaster*. Potts told how Jennet's mother Elizabeth screamed out when her daughter entered the court. Jennet demanded that her mother be removed and then climbed on a table and calmly denounced her as a witch. Her convincing evidence was believed by the jury, and, after a two-day trial, all her family and most of her neighbors were found guilty of causing death or harm by witchcraft. The day after, they were hanged at Gallows Hill.

Pendle Hill

The Witches of Bamberg

The Bamberg witch trials took place in Germany in 1626–1631. They are one of the most famous in European history and resulted in the executions of between 300 and 600 people. The area had been devastated by war, crop failure, famine, and plague, and people were looking for a reason for their ill luck.

Bamberg at the time was a small state ruled by a man with a long name, Prince-Bishop Gottfried Johann Georg II Fuchs von Dornheim! He took a leading role in the witch hunt and earned the nickname "Witch-bishop." He built a "witch-house" complete with torture-chamber. His chief minister was burnt for showing leniency as a judge. The minister confessed that he had seen five mayors of Bamberg at a witches' gathering, and they too were burned. One of them was Johannes Junius, who described the torture and despair he suffered in a letter to his daughter.

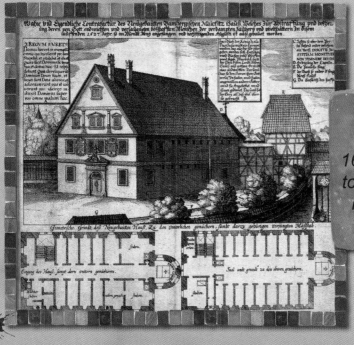

The famous Drudenhaus (witch house) was built in 1627. It is no longer standing today. The torture took place in the half-timbered house on the right.

Johannes Junius at first denied all charges and demanded to confront his accusors. Junius wrote a letter to his daughter and persuaded a guard to smuggle it out of jail and deliver it. He described the hopelessness of his situation. He wrote that he was innocent, but that after weeks of torture his guards had advised him to confess. They had persuaded him that he could not escape and that he would die eventually, so it would be better to confess and end his suffering quickly.

He ended his letter: "Dear child, keep this letter secret so that people do not find it, else I shall be tortured most piteously and the jailers will be beheaded...Good night, for your father Johannes Junius will never see you more. July 24, 1628." Junius finally confessed and was publicly burned to death one month later.

Witch Trials Today

Witch hunts still occur today in societies where belief in magic is common. Some people do still practice witchcraft and believe in pagan religions. Wiccans and druids both stem from early pagan beliefs. Many sections of society believe in the power of healers and ritual magic.

In many societies, a fear of witches still drives periodic witch hunts. Countries including Cameroon, Democratic Republic of the Congo, Gambia, Ghana, Kenya, Sierra Leone, Tanzania, and Zambia have recently been troubled by witch hunts.

Saudi Arabia and Cameroon are the only countries that still have laws against witchcraft, with Saudi Arabia having the death penalty for it. There is no legal definition of witchcraft in Saudi Arabia, but horoscopes and fortune telling are frowned on, and several people have been executed on charges of witchcraft and sorcery in recent years.

Witchcraft allegations are common against older women in Tanzania, particularly in rural areas. Limited understanding of illnesses can result in a family believing it has been bewitched. Widows can often be blamed for their husbands' deaths. Traditional healers are tasked with identifying witches. They usually point to an older, vulnerable woman in the village. Witches are said to have red eyes, common in older women who spent their lifetime cooking for their families over smoky, inefficient stoves using poor quality fuel.

WITCH DOCTORS AND SHAMANS

Belief in witchcraft and sorcery still exists in many societies. Sometimes the sorcerers' healing powers are respected by the community. A witch doctor was not a witch but the person who had remedies to protect others against witchcraft. Shamans are believed to have the power to both cure and kill. Shamanism involves a practitioner going into a kind of trance in order to interact with the spirit world. The shaman communicates with the spirits on behalf of the community. There are practicing shamans in many countries today.

Glossary

blasphemous
Disrespectful to God or to sacred persons or things.

confession
A statement admitting guilt.

delusions
False beliefs that persist despite evidence proving them false and that occur especially in some mentally disturbed states.

effigy
A likeness of a person, for example, a doll made to represent a hated person.

familiars
Animals, such as cats, that embody a supernatural spirit and aid a witch in performing magic.

hallucination
The awareness of something that seems to be experienced but is not real, cannot be sensed by someone else, and is usually the result of mental disorder or the effect of a drug.

heretical
A religious opinion that is opposed to the doctrines of a church.

levied
Established or collected a fine or tax by legal authority.

medium
A person through whom others seek to communicate with the spirits of the dead.

midwives
Women who help other women in childbirth.

pagan
One who follows no religion.

Puritan
A member of a 16th and 17th century Protestant group in England and New England opposing many customs of the Church of England.

retractable
Something that can be drawn or pulled back or in.

supernatural
Relating to an order of existence beyond the visible observable universe, for example a god, demigod, spirit, or devil.

torture
To punish or force someone to do or say something by causing great pain.

For More Information
Books

Deary, Terry. *Witches (Horrible Histories Handbooks)*. Scholastic, 2007.

Pipe, Jim. *You Wouldn't Want to Be a Salem Witch! Bizarre Accusations You'd Rather Not Face*. Franklin Watts, 2009.

Von Zumbusch, Amelie. *The True Story of the Salem Witch Hunts (What Really Happened?)*. PowerKids Press, 2008.

Websites

Fun Trivia: the Witches of Pendle
www.funtrivia.com/en/subtopics/The-Witches-of-Pendle-264233.html
Information about the Pendle witches and an interactive quiz testing what you have learned.

Kids' Questions About the Salem Witch Trials
www.salemwitchmuseum.com/education/worldbook.php
The Education Director at the Salem Witch Museum answers children's questions about the trials.

The Salem Witch Trials
http://kids.nationalgeographic.co.uk/kids/stories/history/salem-witch-trials/
Learn about the witch trials that took place in Salem Village, Massachusetts.

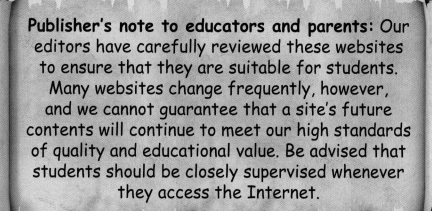

Publisher's note to educators and parents: Our editors have carefully reviewed these websites to ensure that they are suitable for students. Many websites change frequently, however, and we cannot guarantee that a site's future contents will continue to meet our high standards of quality and educational value. Be advised that students should be closely supervised whenever they access the Internet.

Index